WALKING AWAY FROM
IDOLATRY

WES McADAMS

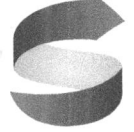

© 2015 by Start2Finish Books

All rights reserved. No part of this publication may be reproduced, stored in a retrieval system, or transmitted in any form or by any means without the prior written permission of the author. The only exception is brief quotations in printed reviews.

ISBN-10: 1941972799
ISBN-13: 978-1941972793

Published by Start2Finish Books
PO Box 660675 #54705
Dallas, TX 75266-0675
www.start2finish.org

Printed in the United States of America

Unless otherwise noted, all Scripture quotations are from The Holy Bible, English Standard Version®, copyright © 2001 by Crossway Bibles, a publishing ministry of Good News Publishers. Used by permission. All rights reserved.

Cover Design: Josh Feit, Evangela.com

CONTENTS

1. The Problem of Idolatry — 5
2. The Idol of Relationships — 14
3. The Idol of Politics — 24
4. The Idol of Work — 32
5. The Idol of Materialism — 40
6. The Idol of Knowledge — 49
7. The Idol of Health — 56

1

THE PROBLEM OF IDOLATRY

PAST PROBLEMS

Moses descended Mt. Sinai with the divine commandments written in God's own hand. He was going to share the words of the I Am who had delivered the children of Israel from slavery with a series of miraculous events that showed his power and his care for his people. However, the delivered Hebrews were not patiently awaiting Moses' return and the words of their Lord. They had given in to their fears and doubts and were violating the very commandments that Moses was bringing to them. A golden calf, made from the materials that God had promised they would leave Egypt with, had become the object of their trust (Exodus 32). When we think of idolatry, we often think of this sight that Moses descended to behold. We understand God's wrath and why it was necessary for him to command that his people should have no other gods before him or make graven images to worship (Exodus 20).

We see God's people continue to struggle with worshipping objects made by the hands of man throughout the Bible. We hear God's continued warnings and his frustration as the kings of Israel continued to turn to idols instead of simply trusting in him. In the New Testament, the apostles preached to Gentiles who worshipped gods of every shape and form. In Athens and other cities, Paul preached Jesus in places consumed with rampant idolatry (Acts 17). People from all cultures and classes were worshiping false gods and idols. What did these counterfeit gods have to offer? Everything, it would seem; promises of everything. Were you seeking love? There was a goddess for that. What about war? There was a god to help with that. Maybe you wanted to ensure a bountiful harvest. Just make an offering, a sacrifice, worship the right god or goddess, and plead for your petition to be heard. There were gods who were worshipped as the patron deity of a nation, a people, a tribe, or a city. There were gods for everything—a god for every topic and a promise for every desire.

But the worship, the sacrifices, and the pleadings of these people to these gods failed to grant the petitioners their needs and desires. As a god among many, these idols were unable to provide results. Did worshipping the god of war assure victory and lasting peace? Did the misplaced faith of the people change the outcome of the battle? Of course not! And not only did they fail in their ability to answer petitions in this life, they failed in their ability to provide salvation in the next. Whether in war or peace, death is guaranteed to everyone eventually, and no god of war can save the soul of its soldiers. In the end, these idols failed their ancient worshippers.

- How many idols can you think of that are named in the Bible?
- How can your knowledge of idol worship from history or literature add to your understanding of the reasons these people worshipped idols?
- How many examples can you think of where God warned his people against idol worship?

PRESENT PROBLEMS

Idolatry is something that many believe no longer exists in our culture. The troubling scenarios Moses found when he descended Sinai or that Paul found in Athens are long forgotten, and God's warnings against idol worship are considered by many to be a dusty relic of the past, irrelevant in current Christian discussions. After all, the message of Jesus is one of love and service to one another, and the gospel is a radical contrast to the menu of gods wherein each came with his/her own promises of instant gratification.

So, is there such a thing as modern day idolatry? We know of other religions who worship idols, but Christians certainly do not bow before golden calves or expect a statue to hear their prayers. When asked who they worship and serve, most Christians would sincerely affirm that they are devoted to God. But wherever it is that we look for satisfaction and security, and whatever it is that we devote our time and resources to, that is how we tell where our devotion truly lies. That is how we tell what our god is and what we really worship.

Is God really first in our lives? Our culture is filled with people who are so obsessed with the idea of being loved that they lose themselves trying to find that person or special relationship that will provide what they desire. Others are so devoted to the idea of financial security that they give everything to their job, sacrificing important things like being the spouse, parent, or Christian they should be. For some people, they think they will find the safety, satisfaction, and the worth they seek if they are respected or admired by others. They put their trust and hope in the false promises of this love, or this paycheck, or this profession instead of trusting in the true God who can really save them. They may not even realize that they have started worshipping these gods of love, security, and admiration instead of the God of Heaven.

It's easy to fall into the trap of worshipping things we love. It's a struggle to sustain balance, and keep all the aspects of our lives in the right place. We love coffee, we love our cars, we love our families, and we love our church families. But while all of these are good things, they are not "ultimate things." As Tim Keller puts it, idolatry takes a good thing and makes it an ultimate thing. And if anything other than God is our ultimate thing, then we have an idol problem. I would think that most of us have been guilty at some point of elevating something to the seat of devotion that belongs solely to God. True worship of God is a declaration of our words, followed by our hearts and our actions. It is knowing, believing, loving, and trusting that it is only God that is worthy to be entrusted with our very souls and deserving of our devotion.

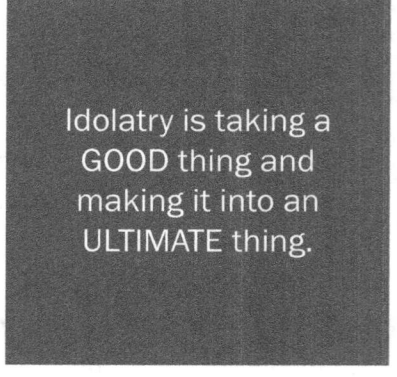

Idolatry is taking a GOOD thing and making it into an ULTIMATE thing.

I've often wondered how Solomon, who was blessed with unrivaled wisdom, riches, hundreds of beautiful women, and access to everything imaginable could be guilty of idol worship. After all, Solomon knew God. He was David's son, and he had communication and blessing directly from God. He carried out the building of the temple to honor God. Yet Solomon yielded to the temptations of idol worship. But his sin was not just in worshiping idols made from wood or gold; he allowed the blessings that God gave him to become ultimate things in his life. Solomon's idol worship began when he let his love for his wives, his search for wisdom, or his pursuit of pleasure take the place of God in his heart. Solomon enjoyed every type of wealth and pleasure, but even he discovered that it all fell short, saying "Vanity of vanities! All is vanity" (Ecclesiastes 1:2). In the end, it was all meaningless because he worshipped the wrong things. Idol worship fails because it is built on a faulty foundation.

- How can placing too much importance on a good thing make it an idol?
- Compare and contrast idol worship today with idol worship of the past.

IDENTIFYING OUR PROBLEMS

To find the idols that we struggle with today, we must search our hearts. If we are to have a right relationship with God, then he is the only one who can sit on the throne of our hearts. Jesus tells us that we cannot serve two masters (Matthew 6:24). Idolatry is taking a created thing, even one that may be necessary and good, and making it an ultimate thing that becomes a master to be served. But how can we identify things that we are placing higher (or equal to) God in our lives? Let us ask ourselves these questions, and then be brave enough to give ourselves honest answers.

- What is it that I am terrified of losing? Financial stability? A certain relationship? My career? My reputation? Some special object?
- What is it that I fantasize about, thinking that my life will be perfect if I could only get "this" or "that"?

Our jobs, relationships, and possessions are all things that are meant to be enjoyed, even cherished. They are blessings from God, and we can use many of these good things to glorify Him if they are kept in the proper place in our hearts. What we must watch for is making these good things ultimate things that we believe we can't live without. We must realize that the only thing a Christian can't really live without is God.

OVERCOMING THE PROBLEMS

READ ROMANS 1:18-32. In v. 20, Paul says God's eternal power has been perceived in the things that have been made. When we look at creation, we should thank the Creator. We should look at these things we love and say, "Thank you, God!" But too often, we let these things squeeze God out, and something else assumes the number one position that belongs to him. Paul goes on to say that people didn't honor or thank God, but instead became foolish, exchanging God's glory for images resembling people or animals, exchanging the truth for a lie, serving the creature rather than the Creator. As Paul continues, the world's immoral choice to worship the created led to unnatural relations contrary to nature. This text clearly states that illicit sexual relations are a form of idolatry. We must be careful to keep God in the ultimate place in our lives, and acknowledge and thank him for all the other good things that are important to us so that we don't find ourselves worshipping the creature rather than the Creator.

The church can be helpful in reinforcing this proper balance: the church helps us with sharing accountability, reminding us that we don't need to put our faith in money, relationships, admiration, friendships, or our country. When we come together to worship God, we bring our pleas, our struggles, and our thankfulness before him. We spend time together reminding ourselves of his greatness and his power, and help each other strengthen our faith in God.

READ COLOSSIANS 3:2-4. Paul advises us to set our minds on things above with Christ, forgetting about earthly things that are only temporary; while we, with Christ, are eternal. If we behave as if our job, football, family, country, sex, or money is defined as "our life," then we need to recognize that as a problem in our life. If anything except Christ is "our life," we've lost our balance somewhere along the way. Christ is what life is all about! Love the things you love, but don't let them become ultimate things.

Idolatry is the very heart of sin. Think about the fruit in the Garden of Eden. The satisfaction Eve thought the fruit would bring was more important than her relationship with God. How often are we guilty of the same thing? We sometimes think: If we could just get "it" and keep "it," we would be safe, protected, beautiful, popular, ready for fun and pleasure. We would finally have it!—whatever "it" is. But we need to recognize that Satan will offer us every desire of our heart along with lies that he will bring to us straight from hell. It's much more subtle for him to sneak a good thing into God's place in our hearts than it is to try to get us to bow before a statue. But these things cannot save us, and they can't really even satisfy us. Salvation and satisfaction are found in the Lord alone. Only when we can look at created things and appreciate them in the proper perspective without displacing God can we be free from idolatry. Let us learn to say as Paul did, "God, I can lose all of these things; they are but rubbish to me. All I care about is knowing Christ" (Philippians 3:8).

FOR REFLECTION

1. What types of idols do you believe are most problematic for Christians?

2. According to this lesson, how does something become an idol?

3. How can we keep the good things in life in perspective with what should be our ultimate thing in life (cf. Colossians 3:2-4)?

4. Despite its allure, why does idolatry always fail?

FOR DISCUSSION

1. Read Romans 1:18-32. How is idolatry at the root of every sin?

2. In your past, what good things were you guilty of making an ultimate thing?

3. How did your past idols prove to be inept at saving and satisfying you?

4. What did you do to dethrone those good things and enthrone Christ in their place?

5. How does the church help us combat idolatry in our lives?

2

THE IDOL OF
RELATIONSHIPS

THE HAPPILY-EVER-AFTER SEARCH

Once upon a time, there lived a beautiful princess. She struggled to overcome obstacles in her life, and she grew wise, and kind, and strong, but still she felt her life was missing something. One day, she met a handsome prince, and they shared many adventures together. He understood her, and protected her, and valued her, and she finally felt true happiness. As the birds sang and the forest creatures gathered around, they were married, and they lived happily ever after.

How many stories, movies, songs, and poems do we know that contain the idea that true love is the ultimate goal for happiness in our lives? Little girls begin their lives with these stories, and they play with dolls dreaming of their storybook ending. As they get older, they daydream of the perfect love, the perfect man, the perfect relationship to come. Boys play at being the hero in the stories, and as they get older, they begin searching for that perfect girl that fills the void they feel. Sometimes people spend their entire lives believing that finding true love will be the key to happiness.

And there is certainly happiness and goodness to be found in love! Proverbs 18:22 says, "He who finds a wife finds a good thing and obtains favor from the Lord." However, if we take a relationship and elevate it above God, we have taken that good thing, that created thing, and made it an ultimate thing. If we place such value on a relationship that we believe it becomes something we can't live without and our lives wouldn't work without it, we have allowed that relationship to unseat God in our hearts. It is like we are saying, "I love you God, but it is this person that makes my life worth living."

There is a difference in believing that someone enriches our life vs. feeling like they are our life. When we love someone in a way that God has blessed, and we thank him for that blessing and keep him in that ultimate place in our hearts, then we have a relationship that enriches our lives. But when we seek after that relationship more than we seek after God, we allow that relationship to bump God from the number one spot in our life, and our life becomes about living for that person rather than God, and in so doing, we declare our lack of faith. We may not be worshipping an ancient goddess of love, but we have, perhaps without realizing it, started idolizing that relationship. God requires that we be fully committed to him, and he said so in the commandment Moses brought, saying, "Put no other gods before me" (Exodus 20:3). When we consider idolatry in its many forms, this issue of idolatry, of putting things before God, isn't as simple as it seems. The Bible makes it clear that there is room for only one God. We have to decide if God is our ultimate thing, or is it something/someone else?

- How has our culture contributed to the idea that true love is the ultimate source of happiness? What problems can be found in that idea?
- The Bible certainly encourages us to love one another. The Bible blesses marriage and family and friend-

ship. What are some passages that teach us the proper importance and value of relationships?

THE HAPPILY-EVER-AFTER LIE

When we allow a relationship to become an idol, we are seeking our happiness in others. We are all flawed and imperfect people, and in reality there is no Prince Charming, no perfect relationship. If we base our happiness and well-being on relationships, then we are setting ourselves up for disappointment. If we are seeking a relationship as our source of meaning in life, then what is our meaning while we are searching for that relationship or what about people who never marry? Does being single mean that we don't have good lives, or that we can't be happy, or that our lives are meaningless? It shouldn't, but if we allow the search for that relationship to take God's place in our hearts, then we can certainly begin to feel this way. When marriage is idolized, this is what happens; we change the way we perceive life and set ourselves up for unhappiness.

Finding the blessing of a marriage relationship doesn't mean that the quest for happiness in a relationship will end for some people. After a couple gets married, they often decide they need a baby, and they begin to think that things will be perfect if they have a child. Certainly, children are a blessing from the Lord (Psalm 127:3-5), but when we look to children as our ultimate source of meaning and happiness, then we are moving God aside in our hearts. Sometimes couples have trouble conceiving a child or with a pregnancy. There are other couples who may never be able to have biological children. If they elevated a desire for children above their desire for God, then they may believe their lives are doomed and that they can never be fulfilled and happy people. What an unfair burden to place on a spouse or on a child!

If a couple is blessed with children, they must love and care for their children while taking care not to idolize them or elevate them beyond their abilities. We should be completely devoted to our families, but we must not displace God. When we elevate our children above God and beyond their capacity, we either crush them with unreasonable expectations, trying to make sure they are perfect, or we let them run free with no boundaries and fail to teach them how to behave, to be good citizens, and to worship God. However, if we allow God to be the center of our universe, then we can be great parents.

Other people may believe church relationships will give their lives ultimate meaning. We need to come together to worship as a spiritual family and give our devotion to God. But we all know people disenfranchised from church because of a prior bad experience. They went to a church expecting to be loved, nurtured, welcomed, and supported, but something happened, and they left with hurt feelings. We must remember our congregation is made up of people, and there are no perfect people. We fail and stumble and disappoint each other at times, even those who are our brothers and sisters in Christ. However, if we allow our disappointment over our hurt feelings to keep us from obeying God, then we have moved God from that ultimate position in our lives.

THE HAPPILY-EVER-AFTER TRUTH

Happily ever after may be a misguided thought here on earth, but Christians look to Heaven for an eternity of happiness. When we thank God for the relationships he has granted us, and we allow him to be our meaning for life and the source of our ultimate happiness, we can better cope with the disappointments we face in this life. We need to tell our young people to look to Jesus for their happiness, not other things. They should be encouraged to hide themselves in Jesus to learn to be fully happy, healthy, and joyful without the need for a relationship to be completely satisfied. And then if they do meet someone, they can build a life together based on a healthy foundation. But if they don't meet that special someone, they can live as happy, satisfied, and joyful people. We need to let people know that children aren't a requirement for a full and enriching life. And we need to encourage parents to teach their children how to seek after God. We need to love our church families without relying on the relationships there to be our ultimate source of happiness. We must remember that we are mortal and temporary, and even the best relationships must end for this life at some point. It is only when we have learned to be completely satisfied in ourselves, with God in that proper place in our hearts, that we are able to enter and enjoy quality relationships.

- Matthew 10:37 says, "Whoever loves father or mother more than me is not worthy of me, and whoever loves son or daughter more than me is not worthy of me." How does this verse apply to this discussion of relationships as idols?
- What are some ways we can keep our relationships in the proper perspective?

IDOLIZING A RELATIONSHIP

The Bible doesn't skirt around difficult issues like idolizing relationships.

READ 2 SAMUEL 13:1-19. David's son, Amnon, loved his half-sister, Tamar. However, the love he had for Tamar consumed him. He idolized her, imagining that she would make him fulfilled—so much so that he made himself sick over her. He ends up tricking Tamar into his bedroom and has sex with her against her will. His fanatic worship caused him to violate her, and it was nothing like he had imagined. His disappointed love turned to a hatred that was even stronger than the love he first believed he had.

That is how idols work. We commit everything we have to get something, but then what we have made an ultimate thing doesn't measure up, and we experience a devastating disappointment, realizing that we have hurt others and ourselves. Idols will fail every time because they are based on false premises.

We see the devastating outcomes of idolizing relationships far too often today. Husbands and wives fail to find that ultimate happiness they thought their marriage would bring, and they may fall into the trap of thinking another man or woman will accomplish that goal. A married man gets the idea that a certain woman is what he needs to be happy. He knows it's wrong, but he convinces himself that if he were with her, then everything would be wonderful and that has become his ultimate thing. He sacrifices his marriage through adultery because he allowed that relationship to become more important than obeying God.

When we spend our lives consumed with this idea of a storybook relationship, we are setting ourselves up for disappointment. We may marry the person we've dreamed of all our lives, but that person is human and can never measure up to a life-long dream of perfection. If we have allowed ourselves to base our happiness on this relationship, we will be devastated when we realize that no person can provide what we have spent our life searching for. Even the very best relationships can't sustain being made an ultimate thing. Consider the unreasonable expectations we place on these people we love when we elevate them to a position intended for God. It's not fair to expect them to be responsible for sustaining our happiness, for that was never a job meant for any relationship.

TEARING DOWN THE IDOL

Many of us know the hymn, "Trust and Obey." What a beautiful song that reminds us that God stands ready to carry our sorrows and fears, to share the weight of our heartaches, and to walk with us in our struggles and our joy. Verse four tells us what we must do to receive this blessing: "But we never can prove the delights of his love until all on the altar we lay; for the favor he shows and the joy he bestows are for those who will trust and obey." We are required to be fully committed to God—to lay all on the altar. Abraham proved his love, his commitment, and his faith to God when he was asked to lay his all on the altar.

READ GENESIS 22:1-14. Abraham and Sarah had waited so long for this special baby that was destined to carry on Abraham's line. There is no doubt that Abraham loved Isaac beyond all earthly possessions. But Abraham proved that he did not place his love for Isaac above God when God asked Abraham to demonstrate his devotion by sacrificing Isaac as an offering. He was prepared to obey because his strong faith allowed him to trust in God, even in this terrible situation. In the end, Isaac was spared, and Abraham's faithfulness rewarded.

We cannot enjoy the true favor of God until "all on the altar we lay." We won't know true joy until we hold the things we love, including our relationships, with an open hand and lay them on the altar. Like Abraham, we must trust that "the Lord will provide." Every day, we need to remind ourselves that our life is not about our family, our spouse, or our friends. We must give up our control and trust in God, and only then we will be fully able to enjoy the relationships we have. Without God in his proper place in our hearts, the relationships in our lives can't fully supply what we need and can't be appreciated as they are: wonderful but flawed and temporary. Praise and prayer drives idolatry from our hearts so that when we suffer losses, we learn to grieve—but continue on—with God as our ultimate guide.

In Luke 9:23, Jesus says, "If anyone would come after me, let him deny himself and take up his cross daily and follow me." Jesus told his disciples to count the cost before they decided to follow him, and the cost of following is everything we have and everything we are. It requires a daily commitment of faith to ensure that we keep God in that number one position and don't elevate those in our relationships to an ultimate status. It's not fair to them, and it diminishes us. We must declare our commitment and be willing to say, "Lord, I love you. All that I need is you; not my house, my family, my country, my health, or my will. I lay it all on the altar for you. You alone are my focus, my devotion. I love these people, but I love you more. All that I truly need is you." By keeping God our ultimate relationship, we can find a happily-ever-after ending that will be greater than any fairy tale we could have imagined.

FOR REFLECTION

1. How can relationships become idols in our hearts?

2. Have you been guilty of turning a relationship into an idol? How so?

3. When we base our happiness or satisfaction in life on relationships, what will eventually happen?

4. Why does the idol of relationships fail us?

5. Which relationship in life will never truly let us down?

FOR DISCUSSION

1. Is the church at times guilty of perpetrating the idolatry of relationships? How so?

2. Are individual Christians at times guilty of using the church to pursue the idol of relationships? How so?

3. As he did with Abraham, what has God done in your life to root out the idol of relationships from your heart?

4. How can parents teach their children that relationships are good things, but not ultimate things?

3

THE IDOL OF
POLITICS

PRAYING TO A KING

In ancient times, citizens of many nations regarded their rulers as a form of deity. One of the most well known passages in Daniel gives us the account of King Darius enacting a law that said "whoever makes petition to any god or man for thirty days, except to you, O king, shall be cast into the den of lions" (Daniel 6:7). Daniel was faced with a law requiring him to make his king an idol, to be the recipient of his prayers. Daniel responded to this command by going to his room as soon as the document was signed, and he "prayed and gave thanks before his God, as he had done previously" (Daniel 6:10). Daniel decided that no king, no law, and no threat of punishment would convince him to forsake his allegiance to the one true God.

We are not asked to bow down before a statue of our ruler, to pray to an image of our country, or to worship before our leaders as many citizens of ancient nations were asked or required to do. However, if we place our trust and our security in our leaders, our military, or our country instead of placing our trust in God, we have made politics an idol in our hearts. This form of idolatry is less visible than what Daniel was asked to do, and so it can take root in our hearts slowly and subtly, before we even realize that it is there. If we pour all our hope, faith, and energy into our political ideals, we have taken a good thing and made it an ultimate thing, and our politics have become our god.

PLEADING FOR A KING

Throughout the Bible, God pleaded with his people to trust in him and not in the rulers of the land. In the book of Exodus, we see that Israel grew into a mighty people and God delivered them from a very powerful nation without the need for military strategy. Why did God send ten plagues on Egypt? Wouldn't one plague do? Why did God not simply strike Pharaoh and his soldiers dead? God could have easily and quickly wiped out anyone who persecuted Israel. But he chose to use the chaos caused by the plagues to demonstrate, both to Egypt and to Israel, that strength and power reigned in Heaven, and not in any leader or any nation. The Lord was trying to teach Israel not to put their faith in an earthly kingdom. He wanted them to realize that strength and power belonged to him alone. Even after the Israelites witnessed the plagues, and all the miracles of saving and of provision that God did before them, they were reluctant to trust in God, and would complain that they were better off when they were slaves in Egypt (Exodus 16:3). How many times do we see God pleading with his people, "Trust me. I know who you are. You don't need Egypt. What you need is me. Quit looking back; look to me. Put your strength and hope in me."

Even after Israel finally arrived in Canaan, they were not ready to put their trust in God for their security and guidance. They refused to realize that they were the greatest nation, a people uniquely chosen by the universe's greatest King, and they complained that they needed a king to be great like the other nations (1 Samuel 8:20). So God granted them what they said they wanted, and they got their king (several kings, in fact), but they still weren't happy because they weren't secure. God made laws against a military census and against accumulating horses. He did this as another effort to tell them to stop trusting in the wrong things, to stop idolizing the military. God wanted their hearts! Israel had refuge and shelter. But over and over, they struggled. They were God's kingdom, and if they had just believed in him, trusted in him, and obeyed him, they would have been safe.

READ ISAIAH 30:1-2. Israel continued to make alliances with other nations to feel safer and to attempt to fill the void that only God could fill because they didn't fully trust in the Lord. Generation after generation, God pleaded for Israel to put their trust in him. But they thought they needed a king and alliances to provide their safety. They couldn't see or trust that they were already safe in the shelter of the Almighty because they belonged to him.

- What examples from the Bible or from history can you think of where citizens regarded their rulers as deity (or when the rulers claimed to be deity)? How did the people of the nation respond?
- Discuss how the report of the twelve spies in Numbers 13 illustrates the point of trusting in God vs. trusting in our own strength or abilities. Compare and contrast the attitude of Joshua and Caleb with that of the other Israelites.
- What was God's reasoning for having Gideon send home soldiers in Judges 7? How does that relate to this study?

PATRIOTISM AS KING

Two topics guaranteed to stir up great emotion are religion and politics. But why is that? Why does politics have such power? Why does it make people so intense? Why do they get so angry over one party or another, one ideal or another, one candidate or another? Could it be for some that politics has become their religion? Could their nation have become the object of their worship?

The Bible tells us to pray for our leaders and give them honor (1 Timothy 2: 1-2). We should make an effort to be good citizens and to be involved in our government so that our voices are heard. We certainly should be thankful for the freedoms we have in the nation we live. However, if we place too much trust in our government, in the strength and might of our military, and in our nation, then we can allow our patriotism to become idolatry.

Patriotism is a good thing, but we must be careful that it doesn't become an ultimate thing. We can be patriotic and love our country, but we must be rigorous in making sure we love God more and worship him only. We can pledge allegiance to the flag, but we must pledge our strongest allegiance to Christ, his church, and his Word. We must be careful not to have our love for our nation and our worship out of balance; we must never be more devoted to the kingdom of America than to the kingdom of Christ.

Do we have American idols? Can political parties (e.g. Democrats and Republicans) and political ideals (e.g. freedom and democracy) be idolized and worshipped above God? Yes. Some Christians forfeit their morality to see their candidates or party in office. Our hope and trust shouldn't be so wrapped up in an election that we compromise our morality because we think our candidate is better than the alternative. Is your sense of identity and self-worth tied up in your devotion to a political ideal? Should we be more zealous about political ideals than biblical doctrines? Like the Israelites, we have the propensity to trust in the might of our nation and our earthly strength. We must be careful not to place our trust in our government and to become too anxious or worried about politics.

While we live in this country, we must remember that our citizenship is in Heaven (Philippians 3:20). We are refugees, sojourners, and aliens in this land as we await our final home. The church is God's kingdom today, and no one can take away our citizenship in heaven because it is sealed with Jesus' blood. If the thought of national collapse fills us with dread, then let us remember who we are and Whose we are! Our trust is not in armies, nations, or democracy that will ultimately fail. As Christians, we don't require democracy to have joy. We know that the church will be around longer than this country, or any other country, for we are the children of God. Nations will rise and fall, but the church of Christ is built on the rock (Matthew 16:18), and is a kingdom that is promised never to be destroyed (Daniel 2:44)!

- How can Christians show love for their country without making their country an idol?
- What can Daniel's vision of the statue in Daniel 2 teach us about trusting in the strength of a nation vs. trusting in the strength of God?

PLACING OUR TRUST IN THE KING OF KINGS

David demonstrated the kind of trust that God desires when he faced the giant Goliath. His trust in God was so great that he went into a battle that he knew he could not win based on his own strength or skill. He had faith that God had a purpose and a plan for him. In many of David's psalms, he praises God for successes in battles. However, even David succumbed to the temptation of taking pride in earthly strength when he sinned in numbering Israel (2 Samuel 24, 1 Chronicles 21). David was a man of great faith, and we can learn so much from both his triumphs and his failings as we strive to learn to keep God in that ultimate place in our hearts.

READ PSALM 20. What significance can we find in this psalm that says the king and the military are helpless without God? Although this psalm was written in a different kingdom and in a different time, the truth that nations, kings, presidents, and militaries are helpless without God applies to all places and all times. And just as Jerusalem should have felt secure, we can know our foundation is sound if we trust in the Lord. Someone can take all that we have away, but we will still have our hope and our faith in God.

READ PSALM 33:4-22. We should find hope and strength in knowing that we are chosen. We don't need to put our trust in a president, a king, or a country that will fail us. We know that no army on this earth can destroy the kingdom of God, and with our trust, hope, and faith in the rock, Jesus Christ, we can take comfort in knowing that it doesn't matter who gets elected or what ideals get brought forward.

The freedoms we enjoy are good and our nation is good, but it is not a Christian institution. The only true Christian institution is the church. Let's walk away from idolatry! We don't have to love things less; we just need to love God more. Let's be thankful for our family, our money, our house, and our nation, but let us be careful not to take these good things and turn them into ultimate things. When tempted to pray before the idol of patriotism, let it be said of us, like it was of Daniel, that we have a God whom we serve continually (Daniel 6:20).

FOR REFLECTION

1. What was God trying to say to Israel through the plagues he sent on Egypt?

2. Read Deuteronomy 17:16; 20:1-4. In the Law of Moses, why did God prohibit numbering large armies and buying many horses?

3. Read Deuteronomy 7:1-6. Why was God upset with Israel when she would make alliances with other nations?

4. Though he was a mighty warrior and great king, David wrote about trusting God in Psalms 20 and 33. Why is this significant?

5. What does Psalm 33 say about God's control over the nations?

FOR DISCUSSION

1. How have you seen patriotism and political ideals become an idol, either in your life or someone else's?

2. What does it mean to have nation and worship out of balance?

3. In what ways specifically must Christians show greater allegiance to Christ and his church than to their government or country?

4

THE IDOL OF WORK

LOSING OUR PERSPECTIVE

In the Old Testament, we often read about how much God hates idol worship. God promised blessings to his people if they would only trust and obey him. However, so many times they turned from the God who wanted to bless his people to the worship of idols. Of all the false gods worshipped in Old Testament times, the god Molech was one of the most horrific. This idol was carved with outstretched arms and a furnace for a belly, and its worshippers would lay their sacrifices on the idol's arms and let them slide down into the fire. It is unthinkable that many times the sacrifices given to the idol were the infants of the worshippers. God specifically commanded his people not to give their children in sacrifice to this idol (Leviticus 18:21). God's love is shown for us even before birth—"For you formed my inward parts; you knitted me together in my mother's womb. I praise you, for I am fearfully and wonderfully made" (Psalm 139:13). Why would anyone turn from such a loving, powerful God to a powerless idol of such destruction?

While we would never think of physically offering our family as a sacrifice to an idol, we must be careful not to place all of our energy, time, and focus into our jobs, only one day to look back and see that we sacrificed our family in a different way. How sad would it be to realize that we sacrificed our children on the altar of productivity, or our marriage on the altar of career, or our relationship with God on the altar of job security? There is no doubt that work is a good and a necessary thing. The Bible instructs us to be busy and attentive to our labors (Ecclesiastes 9:10). We are responsible and accountable for working to earn money and providing for our family (1 Timothy 5:8). But in keeping with the definition that we've been using, we must be careful not to let a good thing become an ultimate thing where our work becomes the source of our security and satisfaction. If our work begins to become who we are and what we are all about, it becomes an idol. If it gets to the point that we can't imagine who we are without our jobs, that we think our purpose comes from our career, and that we feel our worth is attached to our work, then we have replaced God in our hearts. We most often define sin as doing bad things, but sin isn't just doing things that are wrong. It's about more than the things we do or fail to do. Sin can be most deceptive when it comes in the form of doing good things, but for the wrong reasons, often for self-serving reasons.

Most of us would never intentionally sacrifice relationships with our families or with God to our jobs. Our motivation for working hard is to provide for our families and to take care of them, and we are happy to give back to God in gratitude. However, the idol of work can use these good intentions to take control of us a little bit at a time so that we don't even realize there has been a change. We may think, "If I just work hard until I get this promotion, then I'll have security and satisfaction." Then when we get it, that promotion comes with additional responsibilities and even more pressure. We have to work harder because now we feel we have to prove ourselves in this new job—and the cycle just continues. Even when we are home, if our minds are focused on work or we have no energy left to engage with our families, then we have allowed work to take a place it is not intended for. If we are praying with our kids or assembling to worship, but our minds are distracted by our Monday morning to do list, can we truly say we are bringing God our best?

We have already established that we have to work to support ourselves and to take care of the business of living. However, if we begin to base our satisfaction, our identity, our hope, and our security on how busy, productive, and successful our careers are—all to the exclusion of God and family—we will end up disappointed. Many times, we may find ourselves working faster and harder, striving for a career goal. While we certainly want to walk in good works and be busy for the Lord, we must realize that our success is not measured by the career goals we meet. We can't sacrifice our families just so the world can see us check something off a list. Do we find ourselves living that way, thinking that if we try harder, stay longer, invest a little more of ourselves, then eventually we will prevail? And the truth is that we may make those career goals, but at what cost?

When someone asks us who we are, what do we say? Our answer reveals the source of our identity; our answer reveals who or what we worship. If we see our career as who we are, and we look to our jobs as our most important source of security, then we are moving God out of the place he wants to hold in our hearts. If our self-worth and personal satisfaction comes from our work, then what happens when we can no longer do that job? It would be easy to feel worthless if that is how we have defined ourselves and our purpose. We cannot live happily under such a system. We must realize that our value doesn't come from what we do or what we produce. We must recognize that our value is inherent as glorious children of God. Once we accept that, we can place our jobs in the proper perspective. Our work can then become fueled by our desire to provide an abundance for the Lord out of gratitude. God and our families can take their rightful places in our hearts when we are no longer slaves to the false god of work, and we will know the satisfaction that comes from the freedom to produce in his Name and to rest in his Name.

- How can we balance our responsibilities to our jobs, to our families, and to God? Why is this so difficult?
- Many people feel that their careers are a big part of their identity. For example, someone in the health care profession may feel that it is part of them to be a care-giver. Are these thoughts always wrong? If not, what would make the difference?

LOOKING TO JESUS

Sometimes we can devote ourselves so fully to work that we sacrifice the other important things in our life. We don't take a break because we have to check just one more thing off our list, and that one last thing leads to another and another. We think we're doing the right thing, but in reality, we are letting down our families and our God. We can find that we enjoy working hard, having a career, and being busy so much that if we take any time off for something else, we feel guilty. If we take a day off to focus on spiritual things, or to spend time with our family, or just to get some rest, would we find ourselves feeling guilty and worthless because we didn't produce anything? If so, that is a clue that our identity is defined by, and our self-worth is measured by, our productivity. Who are we trusting when we think like this? What are we chasing? If we stop to think about it, we know that if we did nothing for the day or didn't check a single thing off our list, the world wouldn't really fall to pieces. And even on our most productive days, do we find that we are only happy for a few moments before we start thinking about tomorrow?

Jesus came, not just to change our behavior or bring a list of rules, but to fundamentally change our hearts. He came so that we could be transformed by the renewing of our minds and spirits (Romans 12:2). What can we learn from Jesus about work? His mission was to fulfill the law of God, to defeat Satan and death, and to bring salvation to all mankind. And he had three earthly years to do it. In those three years, he had to carry out his earthly ministry, to teach his disciples, and to spread his message, all of which laid the foundation for the salvation for the world. Knowing he had such an important task before him and so little time to accomplish it, we see that Jesus started the first forty days of his ministry with fasting and praying in a place of solitude. Jesus spent time healing, teaching, rebuking, comforting, casting out and inviting in, yet he also took time to meet with his disciples sheltered from the crowds, or to spend time in prayer, or to relax with his friends at Bethany.

If it were important for the Lord to take time regularly to rest, how much more important is it for us? We would never consider that Jesus was wasting time when he took time to pray, or rest, or spend time with those closest to him. Why should we think we are wasting time if we take a break for the same things? We should take comfort from his example and learn to value quiet moments of rest. Let us rejoice that in Christ Jesus, we are saved and redeemed as his children, bought with the blood of our Savior. Let this be our primary status, the most important source of our identity, and our knowledge of how much we are worth. Let's no longer be held hostage by a self-imposed list that is destined to fail us.

- How can taking time away from work help us to fulfill our obligations to God and family and still allow us to be a good worker?

- In Luke 10:38-42, we read that Jesus visited the house of Mary and Martha. Discuss the reactions of the sisters in light of this lesson. What did Jesus teach them? Is it easier for you to be a Mary or a Martha? What can I apply to my life from this passage?

LEAVING IT ALL BEHIND

We can fall into the trap of trusting our job, our career, or things we can amass for our security and satisfaction. We can put all our efforts into worker harder to get ahead in the belief that that will make us happy.

READ ECCLESIASTES 2:18-26. Solomon despaired at his discovery that all he had worked hard for would go to those who had not lifted a finger. Solomon continues his thoughts saying, "Again, I saw vanity under the sun: one person who has no other, either son or brother, yet there is no end to all his toil, and his eyes are never satisfied with riches, so that he never asks, 'For whom am I toiling and depriving myself of pleasure?' This also is vanity and an unhappy business" (Ecclesiastes 4:7-8). Solomon says if we put all our efforts into work, then one day we will wake up and find it is worthless, and that it's all going to be gone. And in the meantime, we've sacrificed what is worth much—our families. Solomon learned focusing on work and accomplishments was all meaningless without God because in the end, it will all be left behind. We must realize that security and satisfaction will never be found if we are chasing after the wind because nothing under the sun can save or satisfy us. In Psalm 40, we are told, "Blessed is the man who makes the Lord his trust." Let our trust in God be our source of security, self-worth, and identity. Let us be thankful for our jobs, and let our work remain a good thing, kept in the proper perspective in our life, so that it doesn't take over and become an ultimate thing. Let our work be to provide for our families, to fulfill God's instructions, and to glorify God.

FOR REFLECTION

1. Have you had a friend or family member that elevated work over their relationships with God and others? How did that make you feel? Did it adversely affect your relationship with that person? How so?

2. Though his earthly ministry lasted only three years, what did Jesus do to keep work from becoming a god?

3. How can work become our identity to an unhealthy extreme?

4. What should be the ultimate source of a Christian's identity?

5. Why does work, on its own, ultimately fail to give us security and satisfaction?

FOR DISCUSSION

1. What all does the Bible have to say about work?

2. How can an addiction to work ultimately rob us of our joy?

3. How can a Christian develop a healthy work ethic without turning work into an idol?

5

THE IDOL OF
MATERIALISM

THE SORROWFUL LIFE

I wonder what it would have been like to talk face to face with Jesus. What would it be like to have a conversation with the one who could see into your heart? Would we be comforted, knowing that he could see an honest desire to serve and follow him? Or would we be hoping that he wouldn't notice our deepest secrets? Jesus talked to a young man that was like so many of us during his ministry. This young man wanted to know what he could do to gain eternal life. He wasn't a murderer or an adulterer; he wasn't a thief, and he wasn't dishonest; he honored his parents, and he was kind to his neighbors. He tried to be a good man and do what was right, and he was ready to do even more, so he asked Jesus, "What do I still lack?" (Matthew 19:20). Because Jesus knew his heart, he knew what would prevent this man from being fully devoted to him. He asked him to go sell all that he had and give it to the poor and come and follow him. He wanted him to exchange his temporary earthly treasures for eternal treasures in heaven, but "when the young man heard this he went away sorrowful, for he had great possessions" (Matthew 19:22).

I wonder if this man knew that his possessions were more important to Jesus before Jesus asked him to sell them? I wonder if he hoped Jesus wouldn't see his love for material things deep within his heart? Perhaps he knew he struggled with materialism, but he hoped that all the other commands he had obeyed would be enough. But what I wonder most of all is what would Jesus see if he looked into my heart. Would I be willing to give up everything and follow him, or would I go away sorrowful?

One of the obstacles in addressing modern day idolatry is our reluctance to believe it is real. We tend not to believe that each of us must address this issue daily. We can see how the possessions of the rich young ruler were more important to him than Jesus, but do we acknowledge that each time we pursue something else for our security, we are guilty of slighting God? We may be willing to say that the rich man idolized his possessions, but would we recognize the same problem in our own lives? Naturally, most of us don't believe that we are really idolaters, yet there is no doubt that many of us have certain materialistic traits, that if not managed, could quickly get out of control. The Bible warns us over and over about worshipping our possessions, but it's hard for us to think we covet or desire things at a level that would meet the standard of idolatry. It can be hard to recognize the difference between enjoying and appreciating our possessions and turning them into an ultimate thing that we place above God. Recognizing an idol of materialism can be far more difficult than recognizing the worship of a carved image or the temple of a false god.

However, if God doesn't fully satisfy us, if we are looking for something more, then often times those are signs that we have a problem. God wants to be everything we need—our provider and sustainer. He told the Israelites in Exodus 20:3, "You shall have no other gods before me." That seems simple enough, but we complicate it rapidly when we try to lean on something else. We can't place God in our lives just anywhere. He won't settle for anything less than the ultimate spot. He does not and will not compete with anything else, and that includes our piles of stuff.

- Compare the rich young ruler with those that did decide to follow Jesus. What did they leave to follow him?
- Discuss what Jesus said about a rich man entering the kingdom in Matthew 19:23-30.
- Judas followed Jesus, but did he have a problem with materialism? What passages in the Bible support your answer?

THE GOOD LIFE?

Most of us don't think of ourselves as rich. But just think of all the conveniences that most of us in our country take for granted that the rich young ruler (or anyone in his time) would never have. We don't think of ourselves as physically rich because it is easy for us to focus more on the things we don't have rather than the things we do have. We see things that we think we must have, and we can become slaves to that attitude of always wanting something more. We often find ourselves comparing ourselves to others based on our possessions, and usually we are comparing ourselves to those who have more than us.

Many people struggle leading up to the holiday season. We can fall into the trap of feeling like horrible parents if we can't give our children all that they want. This travesty begins with the early fall advertising and lasts through Christmas. The stars of the advertising industry work to make our children believe that they must have it all—and to make us believe that we are failed parents if we don't provide it. But this is wrong on so many levels! How many of us begin worshipping at the altar of materialism without realizing it by trying to provide some idea in our minds of the perfect holiday. And even if we are able to give our children all that they might want, should we? We need to remind ourselves that the number of presents or the bounty of food on the holiday table is not the definition of good parenting. We can enjoy being able to give our children gifts, but we need to make sure that we are teaching them that happiness isn't measured in the gifts we receive. Parenting to be popular, allowing the acquisition of things to define us, and letting our identity be defined by our money will fail us, and indirectly, fail our children. We want to teach them that true happiness will only come from knowing the Lord and being satisfied in God. Instead of apologizing because we can't give them more things, let's try to teach them to appreciate the blessings, both material and non-material, that we can give them. When we put God in that first position, we are able to see the world from a different perspective and recognize the vanity of eternal beings putting so much emphasis on temporary things. We must make our actions match our words. Let us sing God's praises, and let our actions and lives say that God is enough.

This problem doesn't exist just during the holidays, though. We can find ourselves grazing for food in the kitchen, choosing one thing and then another, but never feeing satisfied—we just end up with an upset stomach, but we aren't ever really fulfilled? This is what materialism does. Hungry people are grumpy people! We can see an example of that in the Israelites in the wilderness. Despite all God had done to bring them out of Egypt, they still did not trust in him to care for them and began complaining and comparing what they didn't have to what they did have when they were in Egypt (while conveniently forgetting the hardships they also suffered while they were there). In a show of power and divine care, God faithfully sent them manna to eat. But it wasn't long before the manna was not enough, and they started complaining about it (Exodus 16, Numbers 11). They were dissatisfied at what they should have been thankful for. How many times are we guilty of the same thing? If we hunger for worldly things, we will never be satisfied. Taking good things and making them ultimate things will only leave us constantly searching for more.

Our language is filled with words of desiring more or attempting to find happiness in the accumulation of possessions. Think about the word *life*. I'm sure we've all said or heard phrases similar to "Ah, this is living. This is the life. Oh, to the good life." What is usually happening when we say those words? Did we just leave a worship service or a peaceful hour of prayer? Were we enjoying time with family or friends? Maybe. But odds are, those words were said as we were celebrating a new acquisition. Perhaps we'd purchased something that supported our identity, or something we bought that fed our security—this "good life" image that many of us are chasing. Many of us use words to say that God is first in our hearts, yet we find ourselves hungering for something more, yearning for something to supplement what we already have, feeling at times as if what we have is not enough. We may not realize that our words or our hearts are stating our lack of trust in God.

- When did you last say to yourself something like, "Ah, this is the good life"? What were you doing or enjoying at the time?
- Explain this statement: "Hungry people are grumpy people."

THE CONTENT LIFE

In 2 Corinthians 12:9, Paul was told, "My grace is sufficient for you." Each one of us needs to hear those words. We need to be reminded that God and his grace are enough. We don't need to supplement it with something else, but we do need to work on getting things in the right order. This can be a little easier as we worship with our brethren, but as the week wears on, the stresses in our life crop up and uncertainty creeps in. Whispers from others or from our own hearts fuel our insecurities, and sometimes we find that Sunday morning confidence waning. When this happens, do we turn to God's Word, and to prayer, and to our brethren for strength or do we turn to our possessions? Do we find that security, identity, and safety that we seek in our possessions as we seek to bring control and order into our world? Things happen all around us to remind us how temporal this world is, and we know that our possessions can't make us safe. But sometimes we find it easier to trust in our tangible assets for solace during our times of uncertainty than to trust in something that we can't see with our eyes and hold in our hands.

The whole Bible comes down to the concept of being satisfied in God.

READ 1 TIMOTHY 6:1-9. In this passage, we find that even slaves and prisoners can have peace if they are satisfied in God. When we have peace, we don't feel the need to have anything else. When I see grumpy people—people filled with strife and quarreling because they are deprived of the truth—I think they are starving spiritually. They are starving for security, peace, and joy that can only come from God.

If we have a firm foundation of trust in the Lord, then we can find contentment, knowing our needs will be met. It is not wrong to enjoy our stuff or want for things at times, as long as those things are kept in perspective. A man could have a giant house and 25 cars and be miserable without Jesus because he hasn't learned that it is "godliness with contentment" that is "great gain" (1 Timothy 6:6). We see that the rich young ruler had many possessions, but yet he left sorrowful. He chose his possessions over following Jesus, but they still didn't bring him happiness. If we spend our time chasing things, we miss out on the real "good life" that is only found in the contentment that comes when Jesus is enthroned in his proper place in our hearts. Life is about God first, and then all these other things may follow (Matthew 5:33). When we truly see and appreciate God, we can see the abundance we enjoy in the "good life" God has granted us.

FOR REFLECTION

1. What types of things do you spend a lot of time anticipating, planning, and researching to buy?

2. What was the last thing you bought and had the thought, "If I buy this, I'll be satisfied?" When you bought it, how long did the satisfaction last?

3. What are we communicating to God when our lives become all about the accumulation of stuff?

4. How can you enjoy life in ways that do not rely on material things?

FOR DISCUSSION

1. How can the church become guilty of worshiping the idol of materialism?

2. What does Paul mean when he says godliness with contentment is great gain?

3. How can parents train their children to avoid the accumulation and worship of stuff?

4. What one thing do you need to do this week to evict the idol of materialism from your heart and enthrone Christ in its place?

5. 1 Timothy 6:10 says, "For the love of money is a root of all kinds of evils. It is through this craving that some have wandered away from the faith and pierced themselves with many pangs." How does this verse relate to this lesson?

6. How can comparing ourselves to others rob us of peace and satisfaction. How can it cause us to be more materialistic. Why do you think we allow this to happen?

6

THE IDOL OF
KNOWLEDGE

THE PURPOSE OF KNOWLEDGE

Jack had never been anywhere outside his small village, but sometimes he would wonder what it would be like to travel. From a window in his hut, he could see a distant mountain on the horizon, and he thought it would be a wonderful adventure to be able to travel to the very top of that far off place. One morning, he went outside to begin his daily chores and outside his door was a beautiful carriage drawn by two horses. "This carriage will take you anywhere you want to go," the driver said to Jack.

Jack never thought he would actually have the opportunity to go far beyond his village, but he couldn't wait to start on the journey to the mountain he had dreamed of since he was a child. On the way to the mountain, he encountered all sorts of wonderful new sights and sounds as he passed through new places. Jack marveled at the beautiful landscape of trees and rivers and bright flowers along the winding road. When the carriage finally arrived at the top of the mountain, the driver opened the door, and Jack was amazed at the sight of the magnificent castle before him. He was even more astounded when the king came out to greet him and even invited him to eat dinner with him that evening.

During the most wonderful meal Jack had ever tasted, he found out the king was the creator of the carriage, of Jack's village, of everything around him. Jack couldn't believe such a powerful king would have sent the carriage so that he could meet a simple boy from a small village. For a while, Jack listened to the king, and he wanted to learn everything he could about him. But after some time, he began to miss the carriage ride that brought him there. He missed the new sights, the lush scenery, and the excitement of discovering new things, and he decided to leave the castle so that he could enjoy the thrill of the carriage ride again. However, the comfortable and exciting ride began to grow wearisome as the roads got rougher and the villages he passed through looked dingy and ordinary. Although he loved this carriage, he began to feel lost and miserable and, he started to think, "What good is the ability to go anywhere if I have no destination or purpose?" Jack had fallen in love with the carriage and the possibilities he saw with it, and he failed to realize the entire purpose of the carriage was to bring him to the King.

God granted us the gift of knowledge and learning to bring us closer to him. We can use that gift to learn about this amazing world that he created, to build relationships with others, and to teach others about the love of God. However, we can spend such time and effort focusing on learning, and place such trust in attaining worldly knowledge, and find such security in our intelligence that we can turn the good thing of knowledge into an ultimate thing that we place before God. We can idolize knowledge by trusting in what we learn more than we trust in God. The king sent the carriage to Jack so that Jack could come to know the king. However, Jack didn't understand his relationship with the king was the real gift, not the carriage. If we fall in love with knowledge, which is supposed to bring us to God, we can get confused just like Jack did, and end up missing the point and worshipping the carriage. The very reason that God gave us the ability to think, to reason, and to use knowledge was so that we could find our way to him at the castle.

- Why did God give us the ability to think and reason?
- What does it mean to turn knowledge into an idol?
- What do you think Jack learned from his experiences? What can we learn from his story?

THE PURSUIT OF KNOWLEDGE

In 2 Timothy 3:7, Paul talks about people who are always learning but never come to the knowledge of the truth. Many of us know people like this who have become enamored with the idea of being learned. They went off to school and fell in love with learning, but not for a goal or destination. They want to know everything, but toward no end. We want to be a people who will pursue knowledge and keep it in a proper perspective. We can use that knowledge for a purpose or a goal and understand that the ultimate purpose of everything on the planet is to glorify God. We can learn by considering the theories, assumptions, conjectures, opinions, and thoughts placed before us, but we need to always remember that the world's knowledge is not the standard of truth. Let us desire to use the things we learn to help us better understand our jobs, our relationships, and the truths found in God's Word.

Why do people place such trust in knowledge? Some people pursue knowledge so that they will be more powerful. They don't want to know something just to be able to understand better, but so that that they can use the information they have gained to control or manipulate others. Others seek safety and security in knowledge, thinking that if they are smart, then they will be liked or loved. However, this reasoning often fails them because they can be tempted to misuse their knowledge in an effort to prove themselves and become arrogant and prideful. They may want to be liked, but people who are puffed up, conceited, and who talk of only the things that they know often push away the very people that want to be close to them.

If we allow God to be in control of our lives and come to realize our worth based on his love for us, we can learn contentment. What greater knowledge could we gain to help us through this life than that of contentment! Some of the happiest people I know are those that perhaps know the least by the standards of the world. What makes them so happy? They have learned the one thing that matters most: Jesus Christ and him crucified. They know and love Jesus; they know and love truth. Their learning and knowledge have brought them to the mountaintop, and they are satisfied. Unlike Jack in our story, they know the value of being in the presence of the king.

Solomon pursued learning and knowledge, but he came to the conclusion that the pursuit of knowledge would not bring happiness. **READ ECCLESIASTES 1:16-18 & 12:11-14.** Solomon says there is something vexed in the person that pursues and worships knowledge about everything else. There is no end to the books we can study and the things we can spend our time trying to learn, but in the end those things will not bring peace and contentment. Some people have made knowledge their god and science their religion (or history, archaeology, philosophy, or any other study). But these studies can't answer all of life's questions, and this is frustrating to those who worship knowledge, who worship knowing everything.

As Christians, we don't know the answer to every question. There are things about this world and about that next world that we just don't understand. We should always seek to know more about

God, and we should never stop studying his Word. However, we need to be content in knowing there are some questions that we will not be able to answer. Deuteronomy 29:29 says, "The secret things belong to the LORD our God, but the things that are revealed belong to us and to our children forever, that we may do all the words of this law." God tells us that there are things that are not for us to know, but that we will have the knowledge we need to get us through this life and prepare us for the next. For one who worships knowledge, it is difficult to concede that there are secret things that cannot be known. To the faithful Christian, we trust that God has given us access to all the knowledge that we need.

READ 1 CORINTHIANS 1:18-2:16. God tells us that the cross of Jesus will look like foolishness to those who are lost, but those who are saved know it's the power of God (1 Corinthians 1:18). God didn't use the world's definition of the wisest, or strongest, or noblest to carry forth his work. If we begin to make the knowledge of this world our ultimate standard, then things of a spiritual nature will appear to be foolish. But this passage tells us that "the foolishness of God is wiser than men" (1:25).

If we worship knowledge, we become great in our own mind, elevating ourselves and lessening God. Let us desire to know Jesus Christ, to know the will of our Creator, and a knowledge that will bring us to a greater understanding of him. Open Scripture to seek those things that have been revealed to us, his plan and his will for our lives, and don't worry about the hidden things that are not available for us to know. In the story, Jack chose where the carriage took him, but he wasn't satisfied once he arrived there. Let us choose to seek after knowledge that will take us to God, and let us realize the value of being in the presence of the Creator once we are there.

FOR REFLECTION

1. What great truth is missed by many intelligent people?

2. Why are some people so happy, even though they know little according to the world's standards?

3. Why will pursuing knowledge only for knowledge's sake leave us unsatisfied?

FOR DISCUSSION

1. What did Paul mean when he said some people are always learning, but never coming to a knowledge of the truth?

2. In Ecclesiastes, what did Solomon say about pursuing happiness and contentment through knowledge and learning?

3. How is God's wisdom different from the wisdom of the world?

4. Do you believe the Bible answers all our questions? Explain your answer.

5. What do you think are some of the secret things that are unknown to us?

7

THE IDOL OF
HEALTH

SEEING OUTWARD BEAUTY

In ancient Greece, Aphrodite was worshipped as the goddess of beauty. Beauty and love were linked together, and the physical human form was worshipped with statues and temples and offerings made to the goddess. In one myth about Aphrodite, she falls in love with Adonis who to the Greeks, was the personification of masculine beauty. The myths surrounding these idols were filled with jealousies, multiple lovers, scheming, and loss. In our culture, we don't make sculptures to worship an idol in a temple, but we may be worshipping an idol of health and beauty in a different way when we place too much emphasis on our physical bodies. We are constantly shown media images of models and celebrities that present an unreal image of beauty that many of us long to imitate. Our society spends massive amounts of money in the health and beauty markets, and the advertising for those markets appeal to our desires for physical perfection. Even Christians can put aside godly principles of modesty and treating our bodies with respect in favor of fashion and pleasure.

When we learn about the intricate, complex, and precise workings of our bodies, we should be in such awe of the magnificence of our Creator. Certainly, God intends for us to take care of ourselves physically. God gave special dietary instructions as part of the Old Law, and in 1 Corinthians 6:19-20, we are told our body is a temple for the Holy Spirit. We should be good stewards of our bodies, and it is good for us to be healthy—but for what purpose? Our bodies belong to God and are meant to work to glorify him. Our bodies are only a tool, and the value in our bodies is that we can use them to serve and glorify God.

God created us to admire physical beauty. The Bible mentions the beauty of Sarah, Rebekah, Rachel, Esther, Abigail, the daughters of Job, and other women. In the Song of Solomon, Solomon describes in detail the physical beauty of his wife. To admire or desire to be physically beautiful is not wrong if it is kept in the right perspective. However, we must realize that physical beauty fades. If a woman devotes herself only to looking beautiful, then what happens to her when her physical beauty fades? When men value their physical strength too much, where does that leave them when they are no longer strong? Placing all our self-worth in our physical bodies sets us up to be miserable as we age.

READ 2 CORINTHIANS 4:16-18. Paul is talking more about the persecution we endure in our bodies, but it also has application in this lesson. He talks about how our bodies waste away. If we understand that our real value is in heaven, and God's power is renewing our inner self daily, we can be at peace as our appearance deteriorates.

READ 2 CORINTHIANS 5:1-10. The tent that Paul is talking about is our body; so of course, we should take care of it. We want a solid structure to keep the weather out—not for vain reasons, but so that we can serve God. Most people in our culture do not live with the hope and expectation of the resurrection. They idolize their physical beauty and health because they don't have the hope of a better body after this life. As we age and see these changes as Christians, we could despair, but instead, let's accept these things with grace as we look forward to something better. Understanding what is of infinite value (the difference between what is temporary and what is eternal) will allow us to take care of our bodies without going overboard.

- How did ancient Greeks worship the body?
- Do you think we can appreciate physical beauty without making it an idol? Is there a difference? If so, what is it?

SEEKING INWARD BEAUTY

READ 1 TIMOTHY 2:8-10 & 1 PETER 3:1-7. We can see in these passages that God desires us to seek inner beauty more than focusing on our outward appearances. We can allow ourselves to place too much emphasis on physical appearances. Consider a young person who is battling terrible acne, and he becomes so wrapped up in his appearance that it consumes him. He feels that he can't be happy unless he looks a certain way, convinced that his value is based on his appearance. This is a struggle faced by men and women alike of any age. We can become concerned about the color of our hair, or if we have hair at all, or our weight, or the size clothes we wear. A poor self-image can deplete our confidence and keep us focused on ourselves, robbing us of joy and friendships. In 1 Samuel 16, the Lord was to show Samuel which of Jesse's sons he had chosen to be the king of Israel. When Samuel thought the chosen son would be Eliab, the Lord said to Samuel, "Do not look on his appearance or on the height of his stature, because I have rejected him. For the Lord sees not as man sees: man looks on the outward appearance, but the

Lord looks on the heart" (1 Samuel 16:7). If we can learn to look on ourselves and on others the way the Lord does, we would know that our physical appearance ultimately does not provide our value or our worth. Let us strive to make our hearts beautiful, and let us look for a beautiful heart in others.

In 1 Timothy 4:7-10, Paul says that training of our bodies is of some value, but godliness is of value in every way, both in this life and in the one to come. Let us take care that we don't neglect godliness because we have become caught up in focusing on our bodies and our appearance that only have value in this life. Keeping our hope set on a living God, let us be faithful stewards of our bodies. We can do this by being healthy, exercising, and respecting our bodies so that we can serve and glorify him. Unlike Aphrodite, or other false gods with false promises, our God looks at the beauty of the inner man, a beauty that does not promote jealousies and that does not fade with age, and a beauty that can grant contentment in this life and hope for the next.

Have you ever seen a little girl with a dandelion? She thinks she has found the best thing ever. She will drag the yellow flowers around in her little fists to put them in a jar of water or braid them into her hair. When they turn into seeds, she will make silent wishes as she blows the seeds. To her, these little flowers are prized possessions of great value. But what are they really worth? Perhaps priceless in the context of watching the simple innocent joys of a child, but generally dandelions are considered to be weeds and a nuisance. Many people fight hard to get rid of dandelions in their yard, even paying someone to get rid of them. But what if their value changed? What if florists suddenly decided to sell them or brides carried them in their bouquets? What if we decorated with them at certain times of the year or gave them as gifts? What if the world suddenly began to value dandelions?

This is the problem with idolatry: it's when we take something with little value—something that certainly has no eternal value—and assign great worth to it. Worship is declaring our devotion to something, saying it is of infinite value, assigning great worth to it. Whether it is relationships, careers, knowledge, houses, cars, or anything else, we can make them ultimate things, thinking we derive happiness and security from them. Only later do we find that we've been fooled and tricked into investing our hearts in something that turns out to be eternally worthless.

We can fall into the temptation of supplementing our joy, security, and peace of mind with relationships, politics, work, materialism, knowledge, and health. We start to think we can't live without these things or that we wouldn't be happy without them. We would never say that they are more valuable than God in our lives, but if we examine our thoughts and actions, would we find we are placing too much trust and emphasis in these things? In Matthew 13:44, Jesus says the kingdom of heaven is like a man digging in a field. He finds a treasure and realizes its value, so he sells everything he has to go and buy the field and get the treasure. He sells the 99% to get the 1%. Could we do that? Or do we think we need that 99%?

All these things we've studied are good things that help us in our lives on this earth if kept in the proper perspective. However, we can have peace, security, and joy without them if we have Jesus. Like the dandelion, these things are temporary. If we allow the world to influence the value we place on these things, we might find that we've been decorating with dandelions. In Philippians 3:8, Paul said that he considered everything else to be rubbish when compared to the surpassing value of Jesus. If we understand the worship that is due our Savior, we can place all else into the proper perspective.

Most of us don't struggle with worshipping at an altar of a statue, but at times most of us struggle with keeping our priorities focused properly on God. We can make relationships, politics, work, money, knowledge, and health an ultimate thing without realizing it. We must stop and evaluate our hearts, our minds, and our actions to make sure that we are always seeking first the kingdom of God (Matthew 6), and then all the other good and useful things in our lives can be added after that. Let us be grateful for the blessings we are given, and fill our hearts and minds with praise and gratitude to the living, faithful, loving God we serve.

FOR REFLECTION

1. When we spend a lifetime worshipping our bodies, what effect does this have on us in our old age?

2. According to Paul, why is it futile to care too much for our bodies?

3. In his first letter to Timothy, why did Paul express more concern for one's inner self vs. the outer body?

FOR DISCUSSION

1. In what ways do people today worship their bodies?

2. How early in life do people begin to worship their bodies? What negative effects does this lead to?

3. Should Christians take care of their bodies? If so, for what purpose?

4. How can the church show greater appreciation for the inner, eternal part of a person vs. the outer, temporary part?

PERSONAL NOTES

PERSONAL NOTES

PERSONAL NOTES

PERSONAL NOTES

PERSONAL NOTES

PERSONAL NOTES

PERSONAL NOTES

ABOUT THE AUTHOR

WES McADAMS preaches for the Baker Heights Church of Christ in Abilene, TX. He and his wife, Hollee, have two sons. Wes is the author of *The Treasure Chest of Grace* and blogs regularly about various issues concerning New Testament Christianity at RadicallyChristian.com.

To order additional Bible Studies from Start2Finish, visit start2finish.org/bible-studies, call (888) 978-3850, or ask for them at your favorite Christian bookstore.

Also available for Kindle, Nook, & iBooks.

www.ingramcontent.com/pod-product-compliance
Lightning Source LLC
Chambersburg PA
CBHW070104120526
44588CB00034B/2253